ECK METHOD

for

FLUTE

by

EMIL ECK

Belwin Mills
Publishing Corp.

MELVILLE, N. Y. 11746

ED. LIBR.
No. 84

FOREWORD

In preparing this method the writer's aim has been to effect the gradual development of the student both technically and tonally through exercises arranged logically from the standpoint of (a) rhythmic development, (b) gradual extension of range, and (c) development of finger dexterity. Keeping the amount of explanatory material at a minimum, the method of presentation has been left to the instructor who, through his frequent contact with the pupil is best qualified to determine the most efficient procedure.

Melodies have been chosen which lend themselves readily to correct phrasing and, considering the limited technical ability of the pupil, the exercises have been made as melodious as possible avoiding monotony and undue repetition of rhythmic pattern.

Illustration 1. Showing correct adjustment of the head-piece. Be certain the first key is in line with the center of the embouchure hole, as shown.

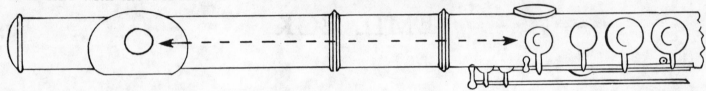

Illustration 2. Showing correct adjustment of the tail-piece. Be certain that the post indicated by the arrow is in line with the center of key no. 3.

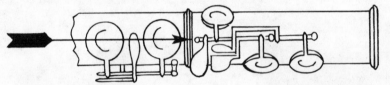

ASSEMBLING THE FLUTE

The flute consists of three parts, head piece, middle piece and end piece. To assemble it, remove the small cap from the middle and take it firmly in your left hand (above the mechanism). Then take the end piece in your right hand (below the mechanism) and attach it to the joint of the middle part by a winding motion to the left. Then remove the small cap from the head piece, take it in your right hand and fit it to the middle part in the same manner as you fitted the end piece. To take the flute apart reverse these movements. Never grasp the flute on its mechanism as this may result in damaging it. The *joints* should be kept clean from dirt or grit. About once a week clean and grease them with joint-grease.

The head piece is fitted with a cork. Its proper place is about seventeen millimeters from the center of the embouchure (the hole in the head piece) to the cork. It can be adjusted by the nut at the end of the piece. Do not disturb the cork. If it is not in its right place the flute will be out of tune. If the first D's are not in tune, the cork is most likely in the wrong place. If you differ in *pitch* with other instruments, pull the head piece out, if you are sharp, push it in if you are flat.

To clean the instrument use a clean cloth or chamois skin. Great care should be exercised inasmuch as the flute mechanism is very delicate. It is advisable to have the flute looked over by a competent repair man about once a year.

THE FIRST LESSON

Take the head piece in your two hands, the end nearest the embouchure, in the palm of your left hand, the other side in the right. Close the two lips lightly and spread them a little as you would when smiling. Then place the embouchure at your lower lip so that you feel the rim of it at a point on the red of the lip just above the white. The center of the rim should be about at the center of the lip. This is not a fast rule. Some experimenting as to position is necessary. (See pictures on page 3).

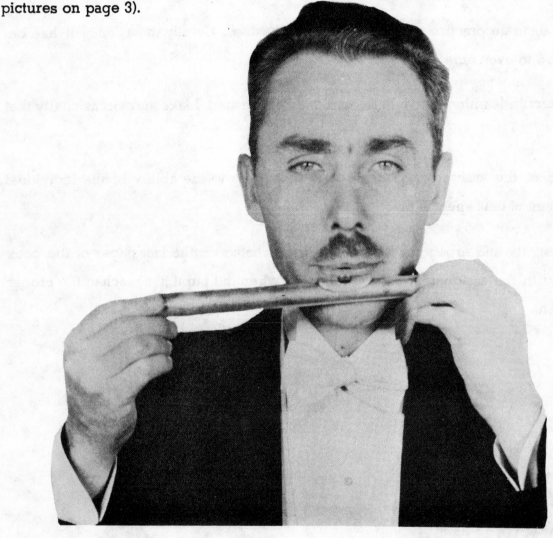

Now we try to produce a sound. Take a good breath and close your lips so as to stop the air from getting out. At the same moment place the tip of the tongue at the edge of the upper teeth. Now withdraw the tongue slightly. Unless willfully held back, the air will flow out through an automatically made opening of the two lips. The opening should be rather small in order to make the air last as long as possible. Direct the air against the outer edge of the embouchure. The splitting of the air-stream when directed against the outer edge of the embouchure produces the sound. It will take some experimenting. Try to get a better sound by turning the embouchure in or out; covering a little more hole or a little less. After the air-stream is all spent, repeat the operation. Don't take too deep a breath and don't press the head piece hard against your jaw. Always play with a relaxed position. That applies to hands, wrists, arms, throat and other facial muscles; only the lips are slightly drawn.

When you have reached the point where you can produce a pleasing sound whenever you try, assemble the instrument as previously outlined, we are now ready for the first exercise. Before proceeding with the exercises, a few suggestions may prove helpful in emphasizing some important points.

(1) Every note not slurred should be started with a definite attack, not by just blowing into the instrument.

(2) Slow and accurate practice cannot be over emphasized. Carelessness, once it has become a habit is hard to overcome.

(3) Be very exact in learning the right fingerings from the start. Make sure occasionally that you are right.

(4) The length of the assignments should vary according to the ability of the individual pupil; also the amount of time spent at practice.

(5) Scales, intervals and arpeggios which have been listed on the last pages of the book should be included in the assignment for daily practice when the pupil has reached the proper stage of development.

Fundamental Exercises

Tones, that is, sounds at a certain pitch are called "Notes". They are written *on* or *be-ween* five lines which are named the "Staff".

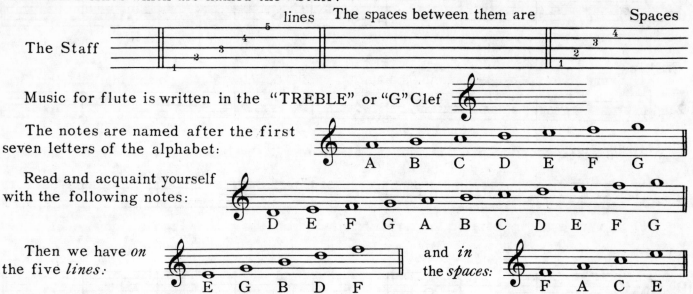

Music for flute is written in the "TREBLE" or "G" Clef

The notes are named after the first seven letters of the alphabet:

Read and acquaint yourself with the following notes:

Then we have *on* the five *lines*: and *in* the *spaces*:

In order to keep time, music is divided into "Measures". At the end of each measure is a line called "Bar", and at the end of the exercise is a double line or "Double Bar."

The symbol 𝄵 stands for 4/4 (four-quarter) rhythm. In this kind of rhythm there are four beats to each measure. A quarter note (♩) receives one beat, a half note (♩)(2 quarters combined) receives two beats, and a whole note (o) receives four beats.

Notes introduced on this page: "Whole" notes, each note receives four beats

* Remember: tongue each note.

Ed. Lib. No. 84-48

6

With no rests between the notes. THINK! Read ahead!

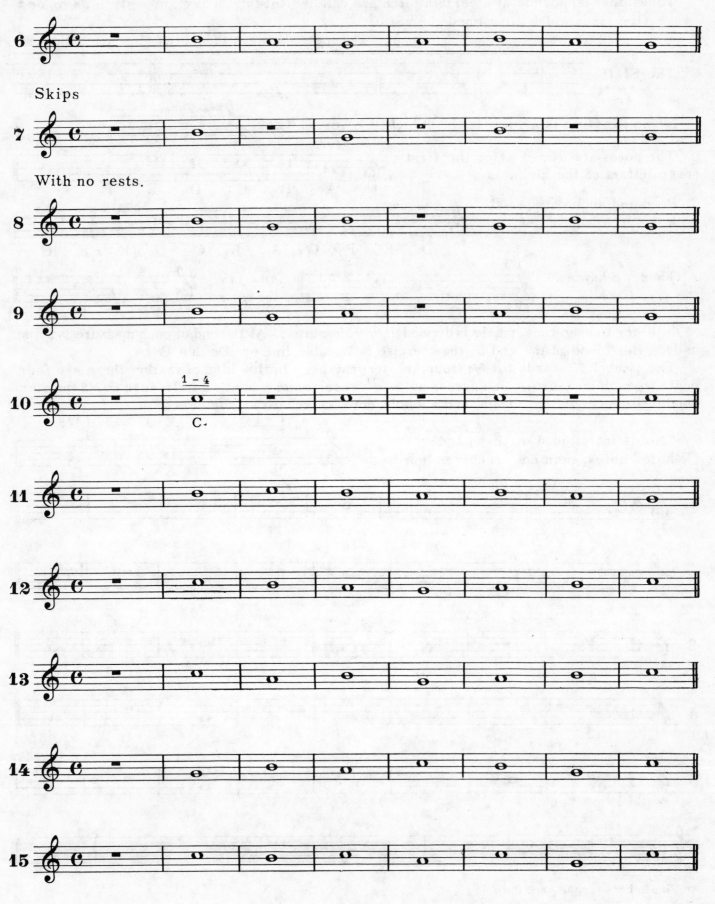

Skips

With no rests.

Half Notes

Each half note receives two beats.

The "C" to "D" change is difficult for the beginner and requires considerable study. Play very slowly and analyse the motion of the fingers.

The notes from E to C♯ inclusive  are fingered like the corresponding notes in the lower octave. To prevent the drop into the lower octave for the "E" the lips should be stretched a little more and the jaw should be brought slightly forward.

The student must not resort to turning the flute towards the body as this will result in covering too much embouchure hole.

Mary Had A Little Lamb

Ed. Lib. No. 84 – 48

Quarter Notes

How many beats does each quarter note get?

A "Dot" *behind* a note increases the note by one-half.

Ed. Lib. No. 84–48

12

A *sharp* raises a note one half step.   The F♯ should always be fingered as follows: $\frac{1\ 2\ 3\ -\ 3\ 4}{T\qquad 4}$

A "Flat" lowers a note one half step.

In Three-Quarter rhythm the quarter note receives one beat as it does in Four Quarter rhythm, but there are *three* beats to the measure as indicated in the time signature (3/4)

A Natural (♮) restores the note to its original pitch.

March

Maestoso

*66 ... simile

The Clock

**68

1 2 3 4 – 4
T
G#

Maestoso means "majestically" and indicates the style. Notes marked with the sign (>) are to be accented, or played with emphasis. The term *simile* means in like manner "or" continue in same style.

**A dot placed under or over a note signifies that the note shall be played "staccato" (separated, detached.)

Ed. Lib. No. 84-48

14

The "Slur" ⌒ or ⌣ connects two or more notes. Only the first of the slurred notes is tongued.

Too   Too

Illinois

Volume markings on this page: *mf* (*mezzo forte*) medium loud. ⟍ gradually louder.
p (*piano*) = soft. ⟋ gradually softer.
diminuendo = gradually softer.

Ed. Lib. No. 84-48

On this page we are introduced to the EIGHTH NOTE. Two eighth notes receive one beat. Study the diagram below and master the rhythm patterns *a, b, c, d, e* and *f* before playing the exercises and melodies.

Song

A *Dot* behind a note lengthens the note by half its value. To a *quarter* note it adds one **eighth** or ½ beat.

America

Different meters

Up to now we had exercises in ¾ and 4/4 time, On this page we are introduced to 3/8, 4/8 and 6/8 time. The *"Eight Note"* is now the unit and receives one beat.

Also staccato

Ed. Lib. No. 84-48

18 The D 𝄞 is fingered $\frac{2\ 3\ -\ 4}{T\ 4}$ the *first* finger left hand and the *first, second* and *third* right hand are *up*.

1

(D)

Intervals

2

Seconds

3

In Thirds

4

Sun of my Soul

5

*Con spirito

6

Jingle Bells   ⌐1 Ending⌐   ⌐2 Ending⌐

7

* In a spirited manner   𝄞 The portion of music between the **double dotted bars is to be repeat**ed.

Key of G

"F" is raised one semi-tone
or one half step.

F# has been previously employed, but we shall now introduce a new *Key signature* (Key of G) in which the F is sharped at all times, unless preceded by a natural(♮). From this point the player must *note carefully* the key in which each exercise is written.

Counting

F major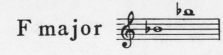

Also the B♭ has been introduced previously. In *F major* the *B* is *lowered* at all times.

How many keys do you know now? What is the signature of G major?

Fermata or hold.
The note is held longer
than its count.

This page is devoted to pattern exercises, Include some of them in your daily study. Chose a slow tempo at first, but keep a steady rhythm. Gradually increase the tempo. Try to transpose some of the exercises for instance play the G major study in F major.

With the increase of the students technic the range should be extended to high G.

★ These progressions are difficult and should be practiced often and careful.

Ed. Lib. No. 84 – 48

D major (F and C are raised one half tone.)

A la Minuet

rit.   a tempo

rit.-ritardando = retarding
rall.-rallentando = holding back
a tempo = in time

rall.   a tempo

Lento (Slow)

*Allegretto giocóso

* Allegretto = moderately fast
  Giocoso = in a playful mood

Ed. Lib. No. 84-48

Some new sharps

This d# is fingered as follows: $\frac{023-1234}{T\ 4}$ Observe: The first finger left is *up*

Eb is fingered and sounds like D#

A# is fingered and sounds like Bb

Ed. Lib. No. 84-48

Alla Breve

Play page and 9 in Alla Breve

Play page 10 in Alla Breve

Review page 13, numbers 64 65 66 and 68 in Alla Breve

Alla Breve *continued*

with Eights

A major

In addition to F♯ and C♯ which we had in the key of D the "G" is raised one half tone.

America, the Beautiful

What Key?

poco f (not quite *f*, a grade between *mf* and *f*)

Ed.lib.No.84-48

28

fz = sforzato, a strong accent.

Ed.lib.No.84-48

Six-Eight Rhythm

with six beats to the measure

(Review page 17)

Six-Eight time with sixteenths. ("Two" sixteenths get one beat)

Ed Lib. No. 84 - 48

Triplets
(Three eighths receive one beat)

Serenade

Schubert

* E♯ is fingered and sounds like F

Ed. Lib. No. 84 – 48

Six-Eight Rhythm
with two beats to the measure

A Folk Song

Study these rhythms

Danish Lullaby

Syncopation

Eb Major  B, E and A are lowered one half step

A Hunting We Will Go

Ed. Lib. No. 84 – 48

Sixteenth Notes

In as much as exercises with Sixteenths require considerably more facility of the tongue and fingers a tempo should be chosen in which they can be performed accurately both as to notes and rhythm.

Ed. Lib. No. 84-48

E major

F, C, G and D are raised
one half step

From 6/8 (to 2 beats)

Ab major

2 3 4-4 (like G#)

Song

Schubert

A common figure in music, and yet one that is often played incorrectly, is the "dotted-eighth followed by a sixteenth." A detailed study of this figure at this point will save the pupil considerable difficulty when it is encountered later in solo or ensemble playing.

First, let us consider the dotted-eighth and sixteenth in *slow* tempo. It is important that the dotted-eighth be sustained as long as *Three* sixteenths, (as shown in the rhythm patterns A-1, A-2 and A-3), and that the sixteenth receive full value. This rule should also be observed in legato playing. The instructor may prefer to approach this problem by the method shown in patterns B-1, B-2 and B-3. Another way which may bring the desired result is to let the student at first play the *dotted-eighth only* with the sixteenth as rest and, at the repetition, the dotted-eighth *and* the sixteenth (as in C-1 and C-2.) With either method, *slow playing* is important in the early stages.

In *faster* tempo, there should be a little more space between the dotted-eighth and the sixteenth, and the latter should be *light* and *short*. The word "crisp" describes the playing of this figure in quick tempo. Attention may be called to the fact that the sixteenth note is more closely connected to the *count which follows* than it is to the count of which it is a part (see illustration below). It is a good policy to give the same amount of stress to the dotted-eighth that you would to a quarter note in a similar exercise.

For example:
more space here ⟶ ⟵ than here

Exercises

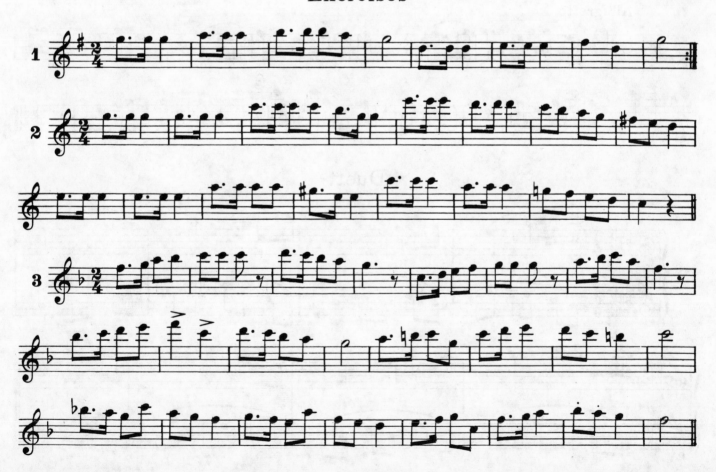

The Star Spangled Banner

Mozart Air

Allegretto

Duett

Ed. Lib. No. 84-48